TAKE JESUS HOME

(The Miracle of Jairus)

By

STEPHEN KATO

ISBN: 9798638419417

First published April 2020

Unless otherwise stated all Scriptures quoted are from the Original King James Version of the Bible – Public Domain

Published by
The Transparent Publishing Company

www.TransparentPublishing.co.uk

Contents

CHAPTER 1 - FEAR NOT, BELIEVE ONLY

[40] *And it came to pass, that, when Jesus was returned, the people gladly received him: for they were all waiting for him.*

[41] *And, behold, there came a man named Jairus, and he was a ruler of the synagogue: and he fell down at Jesus' feet, and besought him that he would come into his house:*

[42] *For he had one only daughter, about twelve years of age, and she lay a dying. But as he went the people thronged him.*

[43] *And a woman having an issue of blood twelve years, which had spent all her living upon physicians, neither could be healed of any,*

[44] *Came behind him, and touched the border of his garment: and immediately her issue of blood stanched.*

[45] *And Jesus said, Who touched me? When all denied, Peter and they that were with him said, Master, the multitude throng thee and press thee, and sayest thou, Who touched me?*

[46] *And Jesus said, Somebody hath touched me: for I perceive that virtue is gone out of me.*

[47] *And when the woman saw that she was not hid, she came trembling, and falling down before him, she declared unto him before all the people for what cause she had touched him, and how she was healed immediately.*

[48] *And he said unto her, Daughter, be of good comfort: thy faith hath made thee whole; go in peace.*

[49] *While he yet spake, there cometh one from the ruler of the synagogue's house, saying to him, Thy daughter is dead; trouble not the Master.*

[50] *But when Jesus heard it, he answered him, saying, Fear not: believe only, and she shall be made whole.*

[51] *And when he came into the house, he suffered no man to go in, save Peter, and James, and John, and the father and the mother of the maiden.*

[52] *And all wept, and bewailed her: but he said, Weep not; she is not dead, but sleepeth.*

[53] *And they laughed him to scorn, knowing that she was dead.*

⁵⁴ *And he put them all out, and took her by the hand, and called, saying, Maid, arise.*
⁵⁵ *And her spirit came again, and she arose straightway: and he commanded to give her meat.*
⁵⁶ *And her parents were astonished: but he charged them that they should tell no man what was done.*
Luke 8

Jesus The Only Hope

In the Scripture we have just read, Jesus was coming back from the country of the Gadarenes. In verse 40, the Bible said, *⁴⁰* *And it came to pass, that, when Jesus was returned, the people gladly received him: for they were all waiting for him.*

As I was thinking about these people who waited for Christ, many questions came into my mind. Why were they waiting for Him? How long did they wait? Who told them that Jesus would be coming back to their region?

And the only answer that came into my spirit was this: Jesus was the *only* hope these people had.

All their hope was in Jesus alone, which is why they did not mind waiting for Him. If we have no hope then the waiting season becomes problematic. Hope is the connector between your dreaming place and the place of fulfilment of your dreams. Hope is the transport from a difficult life to a better one. Hope provides strength and energy through seasons of weakness. Hope is boldness in the midst of negative challenges. It is ever true that people with great victories are people who had great hope. Honor is a product of hope. Self-control is a product of hope too. The day you stop hoping is the day you stop living.

Hope is the reason why these people waited patiently for Jesus. They were driven by hope. Don't you think there were some other people who thought these guys were crazy as they saw them waiting for Jesus? They were probably thinking it was unwise for them to wait. I want you to understand that when you are motivated by hope in God, you will not be understood by most of the people around you.

Opposition will always be there when you are on the way to a great breakthrough in life. Stop trying to please people and begin as much as possible to please God. One of the greatest tragedies in life comes when you care more about that people think and say than you do about what God thinks. When your hope is in God alone, then even when what God has promised you takes long to manifest, you will find grace and be patient enough to wait.

Patience now becomes the driving force of hope in the midst of the powers of opposition battling against you, opening your eyes wide to the rays of adversity flashing against your focus point.

Think about it this way: The focus point is your destination, the transport to your destination is hope and the driver of that transportation is patience.

The waiting season becomes a problem when hope is absent. So also the waiting season becomes heavy and burdensome when patience is lacking. What I mean by this is that patience helps our waiting time to be lighter, it becomes bearable and tolerable. Giving up during delay won't be permitted in your mind when these two graces of hope and patience are operational.

Keep your hope in Jesus alive as you wait patiently for the fulfilment of His promises to you. Taking all things into consideration, including all that God has spoken about your life, these promises will surely come to pass. It's just a matter of time.

Have you ever considered how many people today have called God a liar because they themselves lost hope in God due to a lack of patience? They were not persistent or patient enough to wait or trust in God's timing but instead they created their own idea of what God's timing in their lives should look like. Stop waiting on time but remain waiting on God. Those who wait on time end up frustrated when time passes and nothing has happened. But those who wait on God don't lose focus even when nothing appears to be happening and their hope in Christ is not disappointed.

A Generation with Questions

Ladies and gentlemen, we are living in a generation that has become so difficult to live in. I don't think there have ever been times that are harder than these that we now exist. Let me give you an explanation of why I believe so: we are in a generation where the negative is considered to be more valuable than the positive; where wickedness is now more acceptable than good behavior and righteous values. It seems that everyone living on earth today has more questions than answers. Even those you think may have answers, when you come closer to them, you will find that they have even more unanswered questions than you!

When you talk to those who are now married, you discover they thought that after they became husband and wife that all shall be well. But again you discover that even those who are married, many are wishing that they were not married at all! From the lowest to the highest and from diverse cultures around the world, I have observed that people in their various capacities and roles in life seem to be less than contented with whatever is going on in their lives.

Now you might ask yourself a question: is there anyone who has ever lived a better life in this world? The answer is, "yes". Those who can answer "yes," are only those who are in the world but they are not of the world, i.e. they live their lives not according to the standards of this world but according to

Biblical principles. (John 17:14-16). When you come to understand this mystery, you will stop becoming a victim of circumstances and instead you become victorious in Christ.

Returning to our story we see that is why it was of paramount importance to these people when they gladly received Jesus that they had come to understand that it is only Jesus that can bring a change in their lives. He is the only one with the power and authority to transform their situations.

The very reason they were all waiting for Him is because they had hope in Him. They were driven by the expectation that when Jesus comes,

- He will answer their questions
- He will heal their sicknesses
- He will deliver them from demonic forces
- He will give them peace

They all had hope in Jesus Christ. They had a revelation of Christ, which is not so easy for many people in our generation today. As the Scriptures say:

26 Even the mystery which hath been hid from ages and from generations, but now is made manifest to his saints:
27 To whom God would make known what is the riches of the glory of this mystery among the Gentiles; which is Christ in you, the hope of glory:
28 Whom we preach, warning every man, and teaching every man in all wisdom; that we may present every man perfect in Christ Jesus: Colossians 1

When God helps you and reveals Christ to you, you know that you can live a better life. At first I thought it was for everyone but after I read this Scripture I discovered that it is a mystery made known by the Holy Spirit and through the teaching and preaching of God's word that one may come to the full knowledge of this mystery of Christ the hope of glory in us.

Choose Jesus Christ

Living a hard life is by birth and living a good life is by choice. You can make that choice now before it is too late for you. Your birth circumstances do not define who you are. It is your choice to follow Christ and become His disciple that will change everything in your family, your work and your life situation for the better. With Jesus you can live the best life.

Change is a fact of life, but choice is a principle that determines it. The choices that people make, determine the changes that occur in their lives.

Good choices bring blessings and positive change but bad choices bring about the consequences of negative choices. Everybody is created with an ability to do all things, but we are also given the capacity to choose how and what we live for. Although we are created with the capability to do everything, of course we can't do everything at the same time. We must choose what must be done at any given time and learn how to prioritize our time and our talents in different seasons of our lives.

These good choices are not made as a product of our own good or as a result of a sharp brain or high intellect. No, our good choices have to be a revelation that comes from God. Why? Because it is only God who knows our tomorrow and His plans are always for our good. He gives us the wisdom to make good choices. It is not our own doing.

The biggest percentages of people who fail in life do so because they make choices without God's inspiration. When Jesus is all your hope, it means you are not self-centered; you are not independent but you are dependent on Christ.

Choices taken without God can give you good money but not a good life. That is why you can find those who are very rich but yet without peace. They have all the material things they need, yet they have no true happiness or contentment in the life they live.

This now brings us back to the people in Luke 8:40 who knew that the only hope they had for a better life was to be found in Jesus alone.

In my 25+ years of ministry and travelling the world over I have personally met a lot of people who have great wealth, "living large" as the saying goes today. They have all that they need materially, they are living in prosperous countries but yet it is only those who know Christ who truly enjoy their wealth. Those who don't know Him remain spiritually destitute as the poorest man in the world despite their vast wealth. A life with Christ is a life full of hope, regardless of whether we are materially rich or poor.

The peace that the world is looking for is found in Jesus Christ alone. All the world leaders today are looking for peace in their countries. They have discussed how to achieve peace in all their many meetings and global summits over the years. The more they discuss it, the more they don't get it. Listen to me, today it is only Jesus and Him alone who is the Prince of Peace. Without Him, peace will remain a worthy topic but not an achievement.

Having a great life on earth without peace is like having a great car without fuel. If that vehicle is ever going to move it will require a lot of people to push it. And you can guess how heavy it can be for those who are pushing! That is how a rich man without peace (Christ) is in society. Wealth without good spiritual health is as unproductive as a factory without electricity.

Jesus puts is clearly in the Scriptures, *[15]And he said unto them, Take heed, and beware of covetousness: for a man's life consisteth not in the abundance of the things which he possesseth. Luke 12*

Most people's urgent goal in life is to accumulate wealth and they are willing to do almost anything to achieve their goal. But when you talk to those who appear to have achieved much they don't seem to be contented with their lot and despite all their riches they have something that is still lacking.

Life is not in the abundance of possessions, but in the trust you have in God. Your hope in Jesus Christ and your trust in God is the foundation of every good thing you can ever achieve. Anything built on this foundation brings peace in heart. Those who have decided to put God first, have enjoyed life regardless of where and how they are. There is no life that is meaningful, which is not mindful of God.

Wealth without God is like stew without salt. God is the one that puts taste in every wealth that man acquires. That is why a poor man in the village with God is living a happier and more contended life than a rich man in the city without God.

My twin brother and I often drive to the villages in our native homeland of Uganda, East Africa and we discover people living there who are having a horrible life facing many challenges but yet they are happy.

Conversely, we also meet people in first world countries with a lot of money but yet we find them without joy, apart from those who know God well. In conclusion, what makes a difference in life is God not money.

CHAPTER 2 – TAKE JESUS HOME

[41] And, behold, there came a man named Jairus, and he was a ruler of the synagogue: and he fell down at Jesus' feet, and besought him that he would come into his house:
[42] For he had one only daughter, about twelve years of age, and she lay a dying. But as he went the people thronged him.
Luke 8

In the midst of this great congregation of people who came to wait for Jesus and to gladly receive Him there came a man called Jairus. I love this man Jairus more than the others because he came with an extra prayer: He wanted to take Jesus home to his own house. He had a situation in his home, which he knew only the Lord could fix.

Reflect on this for a moment, as I believe all these other people in the meeting also had situations in their houses just as Jairus did, but only Jairus had the revelation of asking Jesus to come into his house.

Powerful in Public, Powerless At Home

This situation is just like so many people today who attend church meetings, conventions or conferences and meet Jesus there. They get excited at the meeting, they feel happy but then they go back to their homes and meet the same desperate and oppressive situations they left still waiting for them there.

They only find relief and happiness temporarily in church but never permanently at home. They have big titles in church but small titles at home. There is a situation that the devil has planted in their families that causes them to be powerless.

They are extremely powerful publicly but powerless privately. They have an influential public image but yet with a very small private image.

So many people are like this man Jairus. He is a ruler in the synagogue. He enters the church and everyone rises up on their feet to welcome the ruler. Everybody listens when he speaks because he is a man of authority in the synagogue. He is respected in public but yet when he gets home, the devil had taken over his only young girl, tormenting her unceasingly.

Jairus' title couldn't cast this devil out of his daughter. How many great people have you heard of who are like Jairus? The devil has arrested so many children of leaders. They are getting killed off by the enemy at a young age and their parents appear powerless to do anything about it. Where can we find men like Jairus?

Ladies and gentlemen, allow me to address some of these issues that are going on in private. So many people have these:

- Private questions
- Private battles
- Private issues
- Private situations

People are going through so many things and yet according to their public image, they cannot find a way to share about them. People are dancing in churches but yet they are crying in their homes. They are rejoicing in public yet so sad in their relationships.

When you talk about marriage relationships, well it's another story! Some bedrooms have become battle fields and boxing rings. Did you know that private battles are more frequent and of greater intensity many times than those in public? There are some devils that have taken over homes and have taken many people captive.

Some people have just given up and given in and decided to agree with the situation at home. They now call it a "family issue" and justify it by saying, "That's our family behavior!" Or they blame problems on generational characteristics, "Our father was like that;" "Marriage issues in our family are always like that." "In our family everyone has that temper." "We all don't care about our children but yet they grow." "That is just how our family is." Oh my, I don't think that this is the will of God ladies and gentlemen! There must be a man or woman who must fight this and bring it to an end in Jesus' name.

The Example of Jairus

Let's take an example of this man Jairus. He came in the meeting with an extra prayer in his heart. He had determined that this had to go beyond just a "church service." It had to go beyond just a position in church or a title given. It had to do with creating a better relationship with Jesus, beyond the parameters of the church compound.

Jairus had to fall before Jesus on his knees and besought him to go home with him. Look at this ruler, this leader of the synagogue. How many rulers today could do what Jairus did? How many fathers today can look for Jesus and bring Him to their children? Do you know how many children are killed by the devil every year because their parents have refused or been incapable of knowing how to bring Jesus to them?

Jairus had a revelation and knew that if he didn't bring Jesus "now" he would lose his daughter of only twelve years. Ladies and gentlemen, there are situations in your homes and families that only Jesus can change. Education can't change it; your fame and greatness can't change those issues. It's only Jesus who has the authority over everything in heaven and on earth. Take Jesus home like Jairus did. Jesus can change your husband or wife. Jesus can change your children. Take Jesus home! He can change your entire family. Why should you lose it, when Jesus could fix it? If it is beyond your control don't think it is beyond Jesus as well. Remember the Scripture says,

20 Now unto him that is able to do exceeding abundantly above all that we ask or think, according to the power that worketh in us, Ephesians 3

Many times we only depend on our own abilities and we tend to think that because *we* cannot change something, it is therefore impossible for things to change. Yet all these issues we perceive as huge in our own eyes are so easy to handle when Jesus is involved. He is able to do exceedingly and abundantly above all. Think about it. When you come to the knowledge of this truth and then you see other people struggling with their circumstances, you will truly wish they knew how God could help them out if only they chose to trust Him.

Why should you lose your mind over something that Jesus could help you with? Take Jesus in that business. Take Jesus in that dying future. Take Jesus in the hope that is dying in you. Please involve Jesus in it all. Hand over all your worries and all your cares.

6 Humble yourselves therefore under the mighty hand of God, that he may exalt you in due time: 7 Casting all your care upon him; for he careth for you. 1 Peter 5

Take Jesus to Your Place of Need

I totally believe that you can laugh again, you can rise up again. Your marriage can be restored again. I feel Jesus asking you the same question he asked concerning Lazarus,

³⁴ *And said, Where have ye laid him? They said unto him, Lord, come and see. John 11*

The Lord has asked so many people this question, yet they have failed to answer. The proper response to this question, "Where have ye laid him?" is taking Jesus to that place of need.

Do you know the reason why many people can't take Jesus there? It is because they have put it in their mind that it's over and it is now impossible for anyone (even the Lord) to find a solution. Even the sisters of Lazarus in this Scripture thought Jesus was too late. We have to know that when it looks too late to us, this is the time when God shows up to help. He is a God of the last hour. When all hope is gone that is when He shows up.

Martha and Mary, the sisters of Lazarus answered Him and said, "Lord, come and see." In other words, "we have already seen with our eyes and we know how he is right now. But you can also come and see for yourself."

It blesses me when the Lord sees. His eyes are not like our eyes. We only look at the outside but the Lord sees in the inside,   *for the Lord seeth not as man seeth; for man looketh on the outward appearance, but the Lord looketh on the heart. 1 Samuel 16:7b*

It doesn't matter what we see. We need to allow the Lord to see as well, before we draw our own conclusions.

Lazarus was a man who was in the grave for four days, but still Jesus commanded him to rise again when they took the Lord to the place where Lazarus was buried.

Take Jesus home to that place where the devil has been operating from. Always be careful with the reports of your eyes. Also take great care with the reports from the eyes of the people around you.   Our physical conclusions have crippled our spiritual calculations. The way things appear in the physical are not the same way they appear spiritually. Taking Jesus there means you have put your trust in Him. It means you have surrendered all to Him. It means you have allowed Him to be in control.

This is so important to God because He doesn't want to do something that man will have glory in. He always wants to do it alone and all glory goes back to Him alone. That is why He will always allow you to try all possible measures that you have, and when you come to the end of your resources, He comes in. Of course, He has to do what we cannot do. But it's not good for us to think that *He* cannot do what *we* cannot do. Come on! He is God!

CHAPTER 3 – ON THE WAY WITH JESUS

[43] And a woman having an issue of blood twelve years, which had spent all her living upon physicians, neither could be healed of any,
[44] Came behind him, and touched the border of his garment: and immediately her issue of blood stanched.
[45] And Jesus said, Who touched me? When all denied, Peter and they that were with him said, Master, the multitude throng thee and press thee, and sayest thou, Who touched me?
[46] And Jesus said, Somebody hath touched me: for I perceive that virtue is gone out of me.
[47] And when the woman saw that she was not hid, she came trembling, and falling down before him, she declared unto him before all the people for what cause she had touched him, and how she was healed immediately.
[48] And he said unto her, Daughter, be of good comfort: thy faith hath made thee whole; go in peace.
Luke 8

Never Doubt Your Prayers

Jairus' prayer was answered and Jesus agreed to go with him. What a joy! One of the many things I love Jesus for, is that when you pray, He answers. Never doubt your prayers.

Just after the meeting, the whole multitude looked at Jarius going with Jesus to Jairus' house. Imagine the kind of honor Jairus had in the presence of all the people. It is always a great thing to walk with Jesus!

Just imagine if you saw someone walking with your President or your King. This one is not just a king or a President. This is the King of all Kings walking with Jairus. If there is anything that all people should contend for, it is to walk with Jesus.

I see people struggling to walk with these great people of this world. They struggle at least to take a photo with them and hang it in their living room to show everyone that enters into their houses. These days they post it on Facebook for the whole world to see. Please understand me. I have no problem with all that, it's very okay. But I am talking about the Lord of Glory; the Mighty I Am; the Prince of Peace; the Lion of the Tribe of Judah; the King of Kings and the Lord of Lords. Walking with Him! What a privilege! It is a breakthrough in itself.

So the journey began with Jesus going with Jairus to his house. Now as I am talking to you, Jesus is not giving His attention to everybody. In this moment He is now totally focused on going with Jarius. What a blessing that when we turn to Jesus, He focuses his attention on each one of us.

More Blessed To Give Than To Receive

St Luke, the writer of the story doesn't tell us how many miles they had covered on the way so far when the woman of the issue of blood came in. But we just know that on the journey, she came and touched the garment of Jesus. This is happening while Jesus is on route to Jairus' house, from which we can understand that if Jairus had not been taking Jesus to his house, the woman could not have accessed Him.

She is coming to know Jesus because Jairus walked with Christ. Now this is very important for all of us to know: that there are so many people who will be able to access Jesus because we chose to walk with Him. And the most interesting part is that she got her miracle before Jairus got his. To make matters worse after this woman received a miracle from the Jesus of Jairus, she did not even thank Jairus for bringing Jesus. She just went her way. What do you do when you help them and they don't even say thank you?

Are you in the same situation as Jairus? After a long journey with Jesus, some other people are benefitting in your Jesus even before you do! If I could ask you, how many people have benefited in your Jesus since you began a journey to walk with Him?

These are the people we pray for and they receive their miracles and yet us who prayed we have nothing. These people we helped and they succeeded and yet us who helped them we are still struggling. I know your walk with Jesus has blessed a lot of people. You pray for them to get married, Jesus has answered your prayers – they are married and you are still single yourself. You hosted them in your house when they came to the city, you fed them, looked for a job for them, introduced them to your friends. Now after they succeeded they don't even pick your calls. What do you do?

You pastored them when they were so poor; you taught them all the principles of prosperity. Now after they have prospered, they do not even remain in your church. What do you do?

You used to pray together in the group you were leading, right after they got their miracles, they forgot you. What do you do?

It's you that God used to take them to the highest level. But after they got up there, they have no thanks. What do you do?

I have met so many people who are so wounded. They are now tired of helping others. They think people are just using them. Someone told me once, "I am tired of people using me, I have decided never to help people, they have no thanks, they don't remember, they misuse me." I told him, as long as you walk with Jesus get ready to see many people touching Him. You will watch many receive their miracles right before you. Remember you are the one who brought Jesus closer to them. It's because of you that they will all receive, but you must know that <u>they are not using you</u>.

Yes, you can connect them to Christ and they get whatever they needed and they might not even appreciate you for it, but don't you worry about that. The same Jesus who used you to bless them will also bless you as well. Never be offended with someone else's success.

The fact that God used you as a catalyst for their blessing is enough proof to you that you are not small. Their success must be a proof to you that God is with you and that God hears your prayers. Rejoice when you see them pass through your hands and succeed. Bear in mind that the same God will bless you too.

The Woman Who Suffered

The woman of the issue of blood coming in the midst of the way when Jairus was taking Jesus home has so many things we can learn from. Look at the long years she had spent in her trouble. By contrast Jairus had waited but a few hours or at most several days, whilst she had been suffering for twelve years.

She was a total outcast from society and to fall at the feet of Jesus and touch Him when she was "unclean" through her bleeding was a massive step of faith from a woman who did not even have the strength to stand on her two feet. She was touching the Master and yet she was ceremonially unclean.

Her condition did not permit her to touch anyone. She was taboo and to reach out and physically touch even the hem of the garment of Christ was a great risk for this nameless woman but her faith risk was rewarded by Christ.

She had been everywhere and tried everything, and perhaps she had never heard of Jesus till Jairus brought him her way. Her Deliverer was finally before her. She had spent every penny, exhausted every avenue of hope, she was utterly exhausted of hemorrhaging for so many years, bleeding day in and day out, and in agony with the pain, the smell, the discomfort and her banishment from society. She had reached the end of herself and yet now she found the hem of Jesus and in one glorious moment her twelve years of suffering was healed.

She had been so broken, but Jesus made her whole. She had been a woman without peace but Jesus said, "Go in peace". She was a woman who had no friends, no family, no neighbors, but in the moment of her physical healing Jesus also healed her identity. He called her, "Daughter" and this must have meant so much to her, healing her of deep shame and rejection.

Of course, Jairus knew nothing of her story. We can understand he was only intent on taking Jesus home to rescue his only daughter. Jairus only saw someone come and take something from the Master, before he could take the Master to his home but God's perspective on the story is much bigger. Can we see that as we are walking with our Jesus, we are helping others to receive their miracle?

The Mystery of How Christ Lifts Our Faith

The woman had suffered for twelve years and the little daughter of Jairus was also twelve years of age. They were both female, both nameless and both about to die at the same time.

For many years in ministry I was looking for the mystery behind this. I refused to call it a coincidence until one day God revealed it to me and that is when I understood that all things that we meet on the way as we walk with Jesus are not accidental. God pre-planned everything. Let me hope that this won't disturb your theology but let me try to explain it the way I got it. Why the parallel of the twelve years with both the woman and the child?

When Jairus had requested Jesus to come to his house, he was calling the Lord to come and heal his daughter. But yet by the time Jesus will reach his home, the daughter will already have died. Now we have to look at the issue of faith here and how the Lord was graciously helping both Jairus and the woman with the issue of blood.

When Jairus first approached Christ, he had faith for healing but not faith for resurrection of his little girl. She had not died at this point so all the faith he needed was faith for healing. Obviously we understand that faith for healing cannot amount to the level of resurrection faith. Now the message will soon come that his daughter has died, we have to ask how can his faith be lifted from healing faith to resurrection faith? The answer is found on the way: this woman had to come in on the way.

I believe without doubt that Jesus, after seeing the price that Jairus had paid to humble himself and bow down before Him and worship Him, He decided to help Jairus spiritually by healing this woman of the issue of blood before Jairus' daughter was resurrected. Jesus Himself arranged this meeting and I will tell you why: spiritually and indirectly Jesus is communicating a message to Jairus here, that the healing he is looking for can be found just by touching the border of His garment and can be released even without Him knowing much about it. My God this is a full message here.

Jesus is preaching to Jairus indirectly and He wants Jairus to watch and see how it is a small and simple thing for Him to heal somebody. In effect Jesus is saying, "Jairus, It doesn't require me to walk with you all these miles to your house to do what the border of my garment can do. So, as you watch what the border of my garment can do, then you will now know that as the whole of Me enters into your house, it doesn't matter the situation there, you will have all faith even to the level of resurrection."

Let me hope you got this clearly. This woman came to increase the faith of Jairus. You can imagine these "on the way" miracles even today. Yet without us fully understanding the heart of God, they have offended many people after they watch Jesus perform them to others.

Delay is not Denial

Getting envious of those that Jesus has done miracles for and feeling rejected and denied by God is not the right response. The reality is that as human beings, we all want to have our miracle breakthrough before others have it. That selfish element is found in every one of us. But the truth is that in His compassion and wisdom God wants others to receive first and through this our faith will be helped and increased to receive something bigger. *[30] But many that are first shall be last; and the last shall be first. Matthew 19*

If you want to get something bigger from God, allow God to use you first to bless someone else first. That is why you have to give in order to receive. It is a Biblical principle.

[35] I have shewed you all things, how that so laboring ye ought to support the weak, and to remember the words of the Lord Jesus, how he said, It is more blessed to give than to receive. Acts 20

By the way, of the two which one is bigger, healing or resurrection? Of course, it is resurrection. So if you are to get resurrection, first allow others to receive their healing. The problem is that we keep fighting for the less when God is preparing us for the best. Whenever we keep fighting for the lesser, we keep denying ourselves the greater from our God.

The plan of God is to show us and even others that delay is not denial. The fact that other people have received first doesn't necessarily mean that God has forgotten you. It simply means that He has spared the best for last.

[10] And saith unto him, Every man at the beginning doth set forth good wine; and when men have well drunk, then that which is worse: but thou hast kept the good wine until now. John 2

There was no promise from God for you that He will give you first, no! He can choose to begin with someone else, and that doesn't mean He won't give to you as well. We must learn to trust God more when our brothers and sisters are testifying of God's goodness before we testify.

There is no reason to be envious because the same God who provided for them is the same who will give us as well. How can you envy someone who is given a bicycle when God has preparing a motor vehicle for you? The reason why God is beginning with other people is simply because He wants to increase your faith. Other people's miracles have the potential to provoke greater faith in you. Take an example of Abraham and Isaac.

The Example of Abraham and Isaac

Abraham was without children for a long time because his wife Sarah was barren and could not conceive. But after he prayed God opened Sarah's womb and she conceived and they received their son Isaac.

Later when Isaac had been twenty years in marriage without any children, he remembered that he was not the first person in his family to go through what he was experiencing. His father also went through it. The question Isaac is now asking is, "How did my father get out of this?" The answer is that his father Abraham went before God and prayed and God helped him and answered his prayer. In this moment of enquiry Isaac realized he is the product of that very prayer. So now Isaac also had to go before the same God and pray the same prayer and God heard his prayer and blessed him. He got the twins!

Many times I have asked myself a question about these two servants of God, Abraham and Isaac, because although they both prayed to the same God about the same problem they were not given the same answer. Abraham was given one boy whilst Isaac was given two twin boys. Why?

This is what God revealed to me about this. Abraham had no one he looked up to as his example to believe God. He was the first one to have the faith for a child. So because he was the first one, he got one child. But when we come to Isaac, he looked at Abraham as his example to believe and that is why his faith was more solid in God and he received double. I want you now to mark two things happening here:

1. Taking someone who received first as your example and inspiration
2. Receiving at a later date: the glory of the latter shall be greater than the former.

This is so important to understand when God chooses to bless someone ahead of you. He is only setting up a platform for you to receive double. Wow, this blesses me more! But please, can I talk about this platform a bit more?

Many folks have mistaken this platform because we are living in the days where we have a lot of confusing teachings. Most especially when they teach about the spirits and how they influence our lives mentioning such things as a spirit of delay, spirit of rejection or a spirit of hatred. Maybe you have heard something like that before?

Most of these teachings have confused many people when they find you in this very season, when God has set this stage before you. When you watch others testifying; when you attend their wedding parties; when you see them successful. It is easy to believe a lie of the devil when you are in such a season and that God is not going to bless you. Please try as much as possible to be focused on God, not on the situation.

The problem is that we always categorize the situations we go through (mostly the negative ones), to be caused by one source i.e. the devil forgetting that sometimes God is up to something in our lives. God is using the same circumstance we may initially perceive as "negative" to bring about His will and release positive blessings and glory.

At one time I was speaking in a conference and I asked people there, "If we had four people in this meeting who are having a headache, could the cause be the same?" I heard a lot of answers but later they all agreed that the cause can't be the same.

- The first one's cause of headache might be because he didn't take enough water and is dehydrated
- The second one because of stress at his place of work
- The third one because of malaria
- The fourth one because of eye problems and strain on the eyes

Our God is still training people and most of the training grounds He uses the situations we always go through. The symptoms might look the same but there cause is not the same.

Please understand that our relationship with God is not a group relationship but a personal one. Stop categorizing and grouping the things you go through.

As long as you are moving with Jesus, many things will always happen both negative and positive, but the only way you can overcome all peacefully is to fix your attention to Jesus alone. Leave the people alone.

Allow your Jesus to bless people on the way. After all what they need is not what you need. Their needs are different to yours and even if it happens to be the same needs, Jesus' power can never run out.

The truth is we are not all going to receive at the same time, and you are not necessarily supposed to be the first one to receive. The very season that people describe as delay or those who call you out as having a spirit of delay, they have failed to understand it's just a season of preparation. Now ladies and gentlemen this is so important to understand. Preparation looks like delay but *it is not* a spirit of delay.

All people that God will ever use, He will prepare them first. There is no job you will ever be given without showing the certificates of your qualifications of preparation. A person who has been prepared is someone who has qualified. Now this preparation season is what has caused every one of us to have question marks.

So often we mistakenly face the season of preparation negatively instead of positively. Yet these things that we sometimes view negatively are what God is using to prepare us for the better life we are looking for.

No one has lived a great life without a negative past experience helping to shape them for destiny. God is just using those issues that you are going through now to make you great. It might be extremely hard for you to understand it now I know, but when you cross over to the other side you will comprehend it clearly.

Take for example someone who has taken a course in University, which took seven years for them to complete and another person in the same University whose studies lasted for three years. Even though they attended the same University, their qualifications will not be same. So the situation might look the same but the time spent in it matters and the qualification you come out with will depend to a greater extent on the time and effort invested in it.

Taking the example of further education, if you were studying for one year, you would receive a Certificate. If you study for two years, you will be awarded a Diploma. If you study for three to four years you will achieve a Degree and if you continue study beyond this level you will attain a Masters and so on.

Those you see coming out very fast with their Certificates after only one year who begin to work and get some salary will look at you as you begin your second year of study and you are not earning any salary. Do you know what they will say to you? Some of them will try to convince you that you are suffering from a spirit of delay or a spirit of rejection. But the reality is that after you finish your third/fourth year of studies and attain your Degree, your job will not compare with the one with the Certificate and the salary – you will have a better employment with a higher salary than the one who only studied for one year.

Now these "Certificate" Christians are proving a certain point always but you must grow beyond their understanding. The children of Penineah that she gave birth to year after year were not compared to the child of Hannah that she got after many years of tears and delay (1 Samuel 1 and 2). Samuel, the son of Hannah, became the leader of the children of Penineah. I will talk more about the topic of overcoming negative messages and receiving increase of blessing through delay in Chapters 4 and 5.

CHAPTER 4 – ONLY BELIEVE JESUS

⁴⁹ While he yet spake, there cometh one from the ruler of the synagogue's house, saying to him, Thy daughter is dead; trouble not the Master.
⁵⁰ But when Jesus heard it, he answered him, saying, Fear not: believe only, and she shall be made whole.
Luke 8

At the exact same time as Jesus was still talking to the woman whom He had just healed from the issue of blood, someone came with a message from Jairus' household, saying that his daughter was already dead.

Now this is easy to say and easy to hear when the daughter is not yours but think about Jarius who has been fighting for the salvation of his daughter, who is now hearing that she has died. Consider the pain that he felt and the sorrow in his heart. The grief that he felt and the tears he shed. The loss he felt inside and the fear that engulfed him.

Reflect on the questions that he began asking himself, the disappointment he was feeling, the thoughts passing through his mind, the awful dilemma he was in and the confusion and frustration that were threatening to swallow him up.

I mean A LOT of things were going on in his mind after he heard this message. Think about this for a moment. How many times have we heard such messages about things in our own lives that are pronounced "dead" such as our marriages, children, ministries, businesses, homes, future, projects etc.?

Take into account how often we react in the midst of such disappointments. People do a lot of bad stuff! They can end up hating everybody, blaming everyone, accusing everyone. And then, after you see that you have blamed everyone well, you then turn and begin to blame yourself. That's when you discover people want to end their own lives and kill themselves. They perceive that everyone was not there for them, and they were also not there for themselves.

But I like how this situation was handled here by Jesus. We see three people here:

1. The messenger who brought the message from Jairus' house
2. Jairus
3. Jesus Himself

Focus On Jesus Not the Negative Message

I was asking myself a question, why is it that this messenger's name was not recorded in the Scriptures? This is what was revealed to me: we must not concentrate on those who carry negative messages to us. We must not fix our attention on them. It's not necessary for us to know their names because they are not there forever with us. What matters is not who they are, but whose we are.

And look at the timing of the arrival of this messenger; it was at that particular time when Jairus had already found Jesus and they were on the way coming to his house. Just think for instance if the messenger had found Jairus before Jairus had found Jesus! I believe Jairus could have gone back and buried his daughter if this had been the case, but glory be to God that the messengers are always late, meaning the devil is too late to sabotage the plans of God for Jairus and for every child of God. The healing of the woman who bled was the catalyst for Jarius' daughter to be raised from the dead.

You Are Together With Jesus

If that demon wanted to kill your life completely, it couldn't have allowed you to meet Jesus. But now that you have met Jesus on the way, that devil is a loser. It's now too late. Even if your situation worsens, the God we love and serve is so powerful and able to change it for the better. You are not alone now. You are together with Jesus the Miracle Worker. You cannot fight your battles now, Jesus is our fighter.

Never be bothered by the messages brought by these envoys. They can only talk about the things you have lost, but they have no idea about what Jesus is about to do in your life. Let them talk about those things that the devil has done in your life.

But in a short period of time they will talk about the great things that Jesus has done to you and through you. Your better life will not be determined by what people say, but by what God says. One thousand words from people cannot change one word from God.

Learning to Be Silent and Trust God

We can learn a lot from the reaction of Jairus to this message. He just kept silent. Together with all that was going on in his mind, he decided to keep quiet. Can we also learn to keep quiet?

I believe one of the reasons we are failing to come out as victors in our situations is because we talk too much. We always want to give them "a piece of our mind," as the saying goes. Talking much doesn't necessarily mean winning much. No. Winners are believers who trust in God's word.

Sometimes wisdom shall dictate silence. This is not because you have nothing to say. No! At the precise time when you feel you have the greatest point to make, that's usually when you must be quiet all the more. There are times in life when silence becomes the greatest weapon. Look at verse 50, it says, *50 But when Jesus heard it, he answered him, saying, Fear not: believe only, and she shall be made whole. Luke 8*

The person who brought the message, he brought it to Jarius; but when Jesus heard it He also spoke to Jairus. My point here is the message which was brought to Jairus, Jesus heard it. Remember, this wasn't Jesus' message, but He heard it. Ladies and gentlemen, Jesus hears all that people talk about you. There is nothing that people speak about us that Jesus doesn't know. He hears everything and knows everything.

Secondly, the message found Jarius with Jesus. We must ensure that all messengers find us with Jesus. Never allow negative messages to find you when you don't have Jesus. People have ended up believing things that have not helped them in any way because they were not with Jesus when they were told about what they had lost.

The people you hang around with in the season of struggle determine the weight of that struggle and often affect the outcome. Who speaks into your life when you are in such a season? Which kind of messages do you enjoy? Great messages lead to great destinies. That's why the bible said that Jesus answered Jairus, saying, "Fear not." I was asking myself, why didn't Jesus answer the man who brought the message? Instead He answered Jairus. The reason is this - Jesus has no business with those who speak against your future. He has business with you who believed in Him.

Many times we want Jesus to attack our enemies. We want Him to respond to them immediately. But I have come to learn that He has nothing for them, but He has everything for us. Our God knows that if He gets you in a position of believing Him alone, your enemies will sort themselves out later.

We need to get to a place of understanding that it's not about what people say, but what God says. If people have something they are saying about your situation, then you must know that God also has something much more important and strategic to say.

God Always Has the Final Word

The biggest problems come when you fail to understand God's message in the midst of other people's messages about your situation. Yes, all people may be talking about this but ask yourself a question, what does God say about this? Is God also speaking the same message as those other people?

What I know is that our God speaks last. He allows people to speak what they think they know first, and after they finish, God comes in last with a word that changes everything. Now the challenge is who can wait until He speaks? He might not come in at the time you expected but He will come and speak the final word concerning your destiny.

The most painful time is in between the time people spoke and the time God speaks. What do you do when people are speaking so much and your God seems to be so silent? That's why Jesus told Jairus, "Fear not". That season is always a season full of fear. The enemy uses fear to cause trauma in someone's life in such times. Jesus alone is the One with a message that can set you free from it all. Just take an example of Jairus. All his hope was in Jesus. He listened to Him alone. He just believed Jesus alone.

Fear Not

The first and powerful words from Jesus were, "Fear not." When a message like, "fear not" comes to you it means what takes to fear is present. If there was not fear, then there couldn't have been a reason for Jesus to tell Jairus not to be afraid. When someone tells you not to do something it means there is a possibility of doing it. When one says, "Don't go" it means you were to go. When one says, "Don't eat," it means food is there. So when Jesus said, "Don't fear," it means fear was present there in his circumstance. Don't you think this message applies to every one of us today?

Sincerely speaking, fear has been the greatest tool that the devil is using to cause trouble in a lot of lives today. People today fear everything. Husbands fear their wives and the wives fear their husbands; parents fear for their children and children fear for their parents as well. Fear is felt everywhere. Countries fear other countries, religions fear other religions and people fear each other. We are now living in a generation that has no sense of peace. This is all about fear! If there is any time in history that the world needed a message from Jesus, this is the time. The message that is required for these hungry and thirsty souls is, "Don't fear!"

There is a husband or a wife or business man or politician or president who needs to hear this word, "Don't fear." In this generation of terrorism when people are engulfed with fear to travel, when no means of transport is safe, and when no one is trusted then everyone needs to hear this message "don't fear."

Let me tell you something, in this very season of great fear we who have Jesus must understand that we are safe in the shadow of His wings. When we come to the knowledge of understanding this we shall speak like David in Psalms:
⁴ Yea, though I walk through the valley of the shadow of death, I will fear no evil: for thou art with me; thy rod and thy staff they comfort me. Psalm 23

David the writer of this psalm knew this secret that when you have God on your side, in the midst of terror and fear, you will have no reason to fear because God overpowers it all.

Fear has caused many people to fall victim to their circumstances. The devil will always create a situation that will inject fear and make you worship him. Why do you think the furnace of fire had to be kindled seven times hotter for Shedrach, Mesach and Abednego? Why is it that they had to put Daniel in the den of lions?

The king and his cohorts were trying to create a situation that would inject fear into God's servants in order for them to disobey God and worship the devil. This is still the same strategy even now. The devil is just trying to create fear. So it is vitally important for you to understand that these threats are not for us who have God. He is the same God who will deliver you as well.

This is the same thing that happened on the battle field when the children of Israel fought with the Philistines.

When Goliath defied the armies of God the Scriptures say:
8 And he stood and cried unto the armies of Israel, and said unto them, Why are ye come out to set your battle in array? am not I a Philistine, and ye servants to Saul? choose you a man for you, and let him come down to me.
9 If he be able to fight with me, and to kill me, then will we be your servants: but if I prevail against him, and kill him, then shall ye be our servants, and serve us.
10 And the Philistine said, I defy the armies of Israel this day; give me a man, that we may fight together.
11 When Saul and all Israel heard those words of the Philistine, they were dismayed, and greatly afraid. 1 Samuel 17

Look at this huge, tall, strong man called Goliath, the enemy of Israel using the same strategy of throwing threats to the people of God. And the Bible says after the children of Israel heard his words, they were so fearful and dismayed.

For forty days and forty nights they kept running away from this man because of fear. Yet this Goliath whom they feared, didn't even know who they really were. He had no revelation about how great the God of Israel was. He only knew them as servants of Saul and the surprising part is that the children of

Israel also saw themselves as servants of Saul too. They didn't see themselves as servants of God. This is the reason why they kept fearing and running away.

The time you begin to look at yourself as a servant of man, you will continue to fear man. But the time you will see yourself as a servant of God then you won't fear man or the devil any more. Imagine Goliath didn't at any time talk about the God of Israel and the children of Israel also didn't talk about their God to Goliath. Every challenge that causes you to forget God will always cause you to live a life of fear. Look at all people who fear everything – those are the same people who have forgotten their God.

You might ask me a question now, how did David manage to kill Goliath? The answer is that he was the only young man who came to the battle field and remembered God. When David got to the front lines the Scripture says:

23 And as he talked with them, behold, there came up the champion, the Philistine of Gath, Goliath by name, out of the armies of the Philistines, and spake according to the same words: and David heard them.
24 And all the men of Israel, when they saw the man, fled from him, and were sore afraid.
25 And the men of Israel said, Have ye seen this man that is come up? surely to defy Israel is he come up: and it shall be, that the man who killeth him, the king will enrich him with great riches, and will give him his daughter, and make his father's house free in Israel.
26 And David spake to the men that stood by him, saying, What shall be done to the man that killeth this Philistine, and taketh away the reproach from Israel? for who is this uncircumcised Philistine, that he should defy the armies of the living God? 1 Samuel 17

The difference between David and the men of Israel here is that David knew that the army belonged to God. However, the men of Israel only believed that they were servants of Saul.

There is a huge difference! Your identity as a legitimate son and heir of God will be your security in times of intense battles in life and also in seasons of peace.

When Goliath called them servants of Saul and they agreed, that was the beginning of their failure. But David came with the revelation of God and that was his beginning of victory. When he asked a question, *"for who is this uncircumcised Philistine, that he should defy the armies of the living God?* This is the secret that was hidden from all the other men of Israel. They had changed God's army to Saul's army.

When you remove God and put man in His place you begin to fear men. Man becomes a giant when God is not in the army yet the youngest becomes the greatest when God leads the army. The youngest with God will never fear the greatest without God. David, who believed in God, became the deliverer of the men of Israel from the hands of the Philistines. The day you stop believing God, is the day you have declared failure upon your life.

Can we have people like David in this generation? If yes, then these challenges that we are facing will begin to subside. When people are concentrating on how big and great their challenges are we need to have those like David who can see opportunities in these great challenges. Fear covered all the ability in all these men of Israel. Fear neutralized all their strength and the entire victories of war that they had experienced before. Fear caused them to look as nothing in the presence of their enemies. Fear closed their eyes and they couldn't see God anymore.

Believe Only

Jesus told Jairus, "Don't fear" because He knew that if he feared, he could not have recovered the life of his daughter. Secondly, Jesus told Jairus, "Believe only." This means that

Jesus knew that when you are in such a situation of mixed reaction of opinions, you must have a standard of belief in God in order to come out as a victor.

When you get in such a position in your life, you begin to hear a lot of voices from all corners. Believing God alone becomes the only option, if you are to recover what you have lost. Many people in this state of life begin to believe what other people speak about their situation and later become victims of circumstances.

Victory comes when you fix your belief on God alone. When you hear that your daughter is dead, then you must know that it's only God who can change such a situation. When the doctors fail don't think that God has failed also. No, only believe God.

I know it looks crazy many times when we believe God. No wonder Jesus said, "Just believe." It was sounding foolish but yet that's what was going to save Jairus' daughter. God requires our faith in Him if we are going to move Him to restore what we have lost.

[37] For with God nothing shall be impossible. Luke 1

[23] Jesus said unto him, If thou canst believe, all things are possible to him that believeth. Mark 9

[24] Therefore I say unto you, What things soever ye desire, when ye pray, believe that ye receive them, and ye shall have them. Mark 11

Believers are receivers and non-believers are non-receivers. In the Kingdom of God you only receive what you believe. Do you want God to give you something? Believe Him. What you believe determines where you live. When you believe God, God will determine where you will live. When you believe man, man will determine where you will live. It's what you decide to believe that will determine the direction of your life. Even the life you are living right now is a product of the things you used to believe some years ago.

As I told you in the previous chapter, Jesus wanted to increase the faith of Jairus to believe Him for something bigger and greater. When He saw that Jairus' faith is now increased, He himself promised him that she shall be made whole.

I like the word that Jesus uses here. He says she shall be "MADE" whole. This word made is in the past tense of the word ',make,' which means *to create, to form, to fabricate, to compose, to model, to formulate, to assemble*. In other words Jesus is telling Jairus that if you just believe I will do all this for your child.

This was a great assurance that this young girl must be resurrected. Our God offers assurance to believers that He is able to bring back what we have lost. Even if your issues seem to be beyond repair, God doesn't only repair issues, He has power to create something new and better out of old issues. He is able to assemble your pieces together and make you whole and stand again.

CHAPTER 5 – LET JESUS TAKE OVER

⁵¹ And when he came into the house, he suffered no man to go in, save Peter, and James, and John, and the father and the mother of the maiden.
⁵² And all wept, and bewailed her: but he said, Weep not; she is not dead, but sleepeth.
⁵³ And they laughed him to scorn, knowing that she was dead.
⁵⁴ And he put them all out, and took her by the hand, and called, saying, Maid, arise.
⁵⁵ And her spirit came again, and she arose straightway: and he commanded to give her meat.
⁵⁶ And her parents were astonished: but he charged them that they should tell no man what was done.
Luke 8

Jairus' Faith Activated To Another Level

Jesus immediately entered Jairus' house, _after_ Jairus believed the Lord Jesus Christ for the resurrection miracle. Jesus' agenda with the woman of the issue of blood's miracle on the way was to increase Jairus' faith. Immediately this happened to Jairus, the next step was that Jesus entered his house. What you could have called "delay" on the way was working for Jairus' advantage.

The problem we have in our churches today is that believers take God's delay negatively. We always call it the "spirit of delay". Yet in the *period of delay*, Jesus is working on our capacity to have more faith. God is working on our patience. He is working on our character, our attitude and our ability to persist.

Delay will reveal any insecurity, any kind of false motivation and character flaws. You can know a man well when his lunch is delayed. You can know a woman well when her wait for her husband is delayed. It is during such times that the "real" or flawed person shows up. How do you react when you are in this season of delay? We must learn to allow God to work on us and in us when we are in these times of waiting. It will always work for our good.

Delay Creates a Platform for Something Greater

Proper preparation dictates necessary delay. Delay is not a negative thing. It is a positive thing. It really helps someone to get the best. To be delayed is not to be derailed from destiny. As someone once said, delay is not denial. For Jairus to get the miracle of resurrection it took Jesus to delay a bit on the way. If Jesus could have reached there very fast, Jairus would only have received a healing miracle.

Do you remember what Martha told Jesus, *²¹ Then said Martha unto Jesus, Lord, if thou hadst been here, my brother had not died. John 11*

In other words Martha is saying to Jesus, if you didn't delay to come, our brother couldn't have died.

Do you know how many people today are blaming God for the delay? We all need Jesus to show up yesterday. Even if He could have showed up today, we already feel it's already too late. But think about it. If Jesus came when Lazarus was still sick and healed him, could Lazarus' story have been recorded in the Bible? I don't think so. There are a lot of healings that Jesus performed that were not written in the Scriptures. Delay creates a bigger platform for something greater to take place.

Take for example all the women we read of in Scripture who had delayed in giving birth. All the children that they gave birth to after a long time of delay were all powerfully used by God.

- Isaac the son of Abraham and Sarah (Genesis 21)

- Samson the Son of Manoah in the book of Judges 13
- John the Baptist the son of Zechariah and Elizabeth in Luke chapter 1

So many who were delayed to be born; their parents delayed so much to have children but the season of delay created bigger platforms for greater miracles. However much painful waiting proves to be, after God shows up, you will discover that it was worth waiting for. His timing is always perfect.

Anything that you have ever trusted God for and it has taken long to manifest, please keep waiting and don't lose heart. The same God who promised, He will surely fulfil. I know people will come up with their own compositions, but please don't wait upon people, wait upon God and you will never be disappointed.

God Reserves the Best for Last

One of the signs that shows that you are about to become a failure, is impatience. In Kiswahili we call it, *"wasiwasi"*. Anyone with wasiwasi always ends up a failure. Winners are persistent people. Delay doesn't change their focus.

At first before I knew all these facts, I thought that the woman of the issue of blood interrupted the movement of Jesus and caused Him to be late to the house of Jairus so the daughter ended up dying. But it's now I got to discover that it all worked more for Jairus than for the woman. Yes, she got the miracle first, but the one who received last got the best. God has reserved the best for the last.

Jairus was the greatest beneficiary in this whole faith journey. Have you ever been in a position in life and felt like everything is not working for you alone? You watch others, and they all seem to be moving in their favor except you? Feeling like God is very far from you? That's just a season of delay; it should not bother you so much.

All great men and woman have gone through it all. Great people are great products of great challenges. When God begins to develop a great person out of you, He uses delay to allow the process to take place without interference. Never allow people to interpret your delay season because most times they won't know the plan of God behind it.

During this season of delay, God will always be silent. This might cause you to think that He has left you alone, yet He is even more close to you than before. Just remember it works more for you than for anyone else.

Weep Not

What I want you to understand is that Jairus was ready to go and bury his daughter if the news of the death of his daughter found him without Jesus. Even after getting Jesus, he needed this activation of his faith to another level. You see many times when things like this happen Jesus is up to something greater in your life.

After Jairus received according to what Jesus had planned for him, we now see Jesus entering into Jairus' house. But as he entered into the house, I want us to look at something very important. Verse 51 says Jesus suffered no man to go in the house except Peter, John and James and the father and the mother of the maiden. Now the question comes, why?

Why didn't Jesus allow other people even all the other disciples to come in the house with Him? Is Jesus a respecter of persons? Did He not love some? Many questions arose and they used to bother me so much, but we will discover the answer to all these questions when we get inside the house.

The Lord found people inside whom He didn't invite inside and they were crying. He made a statement and said, *she is not dead, but sleepeth* and they all laughed at Him because they knew without a doubt that she was dead. Guess what happened? Jesus chased them all out to go and join those He had already left behind outside.

All these guys who were weeping began to laugh at Him because they knew that she was dead. Look at their reason why they laughed, *because they knew* …People who laugh at you "know" something about you is dead. They know your life is dead, they know your future, marriage, business, and children, your family etc. are looking dead. But they have failed to realize that what they know is not what Jesus knows about you.

Learn to Select a Few

Jesus had to select only a few people to enter with Him into the house. Ladies and gentlemen, we can learn a lot of things from this. When Jesus was healing the woman of the issue of blood, He healed her when everybody was there in the midst of the whole crowd. But for this resurrection miracle, He selected only a few people to be present. A miracle of healing is smaller compared to a miracle of resurrection; which means when God is doing smaller things for people, it doesn't matter the people who are around. However, for really big things to be done by God, it requires some selections.

When you begin to see that all the people around you are interested in what you are about to get, then you know it's too small. Small things are gotten through squeezed places, places where it is too crowded, where everyone must be involved and everyone understands. But when big things are about to happen, no one cares. Everyone runs away from you. No one seems to understand you. You feel like you are left on your own island alone. This must show you that God is about to do something great in your life.

Resurrection takes place when a few selected people are around you. Never try to involve in your issues those that God is taking away from you in that season.

Take Your Mind to the Bigger God

Stop thinking that God has to use a bigger number than He did for someone else. Take your mind from the bigger number of people involved, to the bigger God involved.

Have you heard in our day what they call the 'spirit of rejection'? They have failed to understand this great fact: they are thinking that all people must be involved in their process. Believe it or not there are some things that God will not do in your life until He has separated you from some people. Whether you like it or not, some people must go. Sometimes the crowd must give way for the cloud of glory to cover you up.

Don't Allow Your Crowd to Stand Against Your Cloud

Don't allow your crowd to stand against your cloud. Abraham's story gives us a clear picture of this whole concept. When God told Abraham to go and sacrifice Isaac, his only son from Sarah, the bible says,

4 Then on the third day Abraham lifted up his eyes, and saw the place afar off.
5 And Abraham said unto his young men, Abide ye here with the ass; and I and the lad will go yonder and worship, and come again to you. Genesis 22

Don't seek the crowd's opinion for you to obey God. Learn how to draw a line for the crowd not to cross. Some of our friends must not cross some "crazy" lines in our life. Can you imagine Abraham didn't even tell his wife Sarah about it? What do you think Sarah could have done to Abraham if she knew what he was about to do? You must know how to separate personal issues from family matters. This was between Abraham alone and God. Some people have failed the test of faith because of involving wrong people in their right affairs with God.

What surprises me is that God didn't instruct Abraham not to tell Sarah. It was Abraham who had the wisdom and who knew that this wasn't for Sarah to know about at that time.

Some people can be so dear to you but you must regulate what to tell them and when not to tell them if you are to be in the line of obedience to God.

Sometimes what we call transparency in relationships must be regulated in order to obey God. Unfortunately, some people have been caused to disobey God by their partners.

When Abraham overcame this issue at home, he found the same issue again after three days journey with the servants that he was with. He had to tell them not to go beyond a certain point in order for him to obey God.

- Great things happen when great sacrifices are made
- It takes a great mind for great sacrifices to be made
- So great mind decisions don't need small mind approvals!

The particular point I want us to understand clearly here, is that for some things to be done by Jesus in our lives, we must know that not everybody will be involved. Yes, we have people we call friends, but they must be friends only to a certain point. We must learn how to draw a line for some of them not to go beyond it. Taking everybody everywhere will cripple your faith.

Not everybody can fit everywhere. Some of them are too young spiritually to understand some deeper spiritual matters. Jesus had to leave some disciples outside because they would not have understood what was happening inside the house. There are some deeper things of faith that will be understood by just a few individuals.

She is not Dead but Sleeps

Look at what Jesus said to those who were mourning and crying in the house, *Weep not; she is not dead, but sleepeth.* He spoke this with His understanding, but according to their small understanding, they couldn't understand Him! Now if He had waited for their approval, the daughter couldn't have risen from the dead.

I used to ask myself a question, why did Jesus select only a few to enter with Him into the house? But I discovered that what He did to those He found inside the house is what gave me the answer to my question. He made a statement, *She is not dead, but sleepeth*, and they all laughed at Him. Then He chased them out to join those He had left outside.

This statement, "*she is not dead, but sleepeth*," is what answers it all. Jesus is looking for those who can see 'sleep' in a dead body. It's all about who can see 'sleep' in this dead girl. Those who could see 'sleep' stayed inside but those who could only see her dead were sent out. Those He chased could not see with eyes of faith and they were a stumbling block to the resurrection of Jairus' daughter.

The ones who laughed were afraid and could only see a dead girl. But the Lord was looking for faith; a faith that could describe the young girl's condition as 'sleep' and not death. He is seeking those who can see with spiritual eyes and focus beyond the natural circumstances and take hold of resurrection grace by faith.

The Great Sight of Faith

This selection was all about the great sight of faith. Where others see death, what do you see?

Many people today have failed to get to their place of greatness because of the people they keep close to themselves who will never see anything alive in them. Those who see everything around you to be dead will always cripple your movement to greater heights. Make sure they have limited involvement in your life affairs. Let them be your friends but only to a certain extent.

Dangerous to your Destiny

There are some 'friends' who only see failures in your life; they only see your future dead; your marriage dead; your ministry dead; your business and all that you do dead. Stop keeping them close to yourself. They are dangerous to your destiny.

Get hooked up with those selected few people who see greatness in you. Those valuable few who see life in all that you do, even when you feel all things around you are falling apart and you can't even see where to go. Those extraordinary few who will always give you a word that brings you hope. They can't stop seeing you as successful in all that you do. Keep people around whose uncommon eyes of faith can see life in the 'dead' areas of your life. Let resurrection be seen in their eyes, before it is seen in your life.

Clear the Atmosphere

54 And he put them all out, and took her by the hand, and called, saying, Maid, arise.

Jesus made sure that the only people remaining in the house before He spoke to the dead girl were people of faith. He had to clear the house first of those with little or no faith. Learn to clear the atmosphere first. Get your house ready for something great to happen.

Then He spoke to the dead girl to rise. Some things will never hear the voice of the Master when the atmosphere is not right. We must learn how to clear away other negative voices for the Voice of the Master to be clear. Chase those with no faith out first then you will hear Jesus' voice loud and clear.

This young girl was dead to all other voices but was still alive to the Voice of Christ. Everything in this planet earth will never die to the voice of Christ. The ears of every creature dead or alive hear when Christ speaks. Christ called her back to life and Christ is still calling His people back to life today.

CHAPTER 6 – ARISE!

⁵⁴ And he put them all out, and took her by the hand, and called, saying, Maid, arise.
⁵⁵ And her spirit came again, and she arose straightway: and he commanded to give her meat.
⁵⁶ And her parents were astonished: but he charged them that they should tell no man what was done.
Luke 8

Jesus took the girl of twelve years by the hand and raised her up out of her seemingly impossible circumstances. Jesus will always reach out to us personally and at the end of the time of delay then the suddenly of God will come upon us as it was with the maiden and we will each receive our resurrection miracle from Christ.

Jesus took her hand and her spirit came again and she rose up straight away. There was no further delay, no denial; only the glory of God at work in what was dead now coming alive again. When we take Jesus home to the impossibility of our broken circumstances, He resurrects us and them for His glory as He did for Jairus, the mother and their daughter. The young girl had been lost but was not restored back to her family and the entire family was restored in God.

What Have You Lost?

What have you lost? What do people say about it? Surrender it to Christ. He can change it all for you. He called that young girl and her spirit came again back to her and she arose straight away. Her spirit came back again by the command of Christ.

There are many things that the devil has taken away from people simply because they have not allowed Christ to take over and fight for them. I have come across so many people in this world who have a lot of potential in them. They are people with great talents but they are reduced to nothing because they have not allowed Jesus to help them. Some issues in our lives can only be changed by Jesus alone. If Jesus is not involved in your life, then you will forget the potential you have and your dreams may never be fulfilled.

There is always a time that comes when doctors reach their final diagnosis and treatments; when counsellors have exhausted their experiences and when all friends have come to an end. That is the time when everyone around you becomes a reporter of what is happening to you in a negative wway. That is the time when Christ becomes your only solution. But what pains more is when you get to that time and you don't know Christ. It is my prayer that you seek Him while He may still be found.

The Scriptures talk about the man that trusts in the Lord, *⁷Blessed is the man that trusteth in the LORD, and whose hope the LORD is. ⁸For he shall be as a tree planted by the waters, and that spreadeth out her roots by the river, and shall not see when heat cometh, but her leaf shall be green; and shall not be careful in the year of drought, neither shall cease from yielding fruit. Jeremiah 17*

Rooted in Overflow and Grounded in Greatness

When you put your trust in the Lord and when the Lord is your hope, you will always live a life that is so different from others. You are planted in a very strategic position of bearing fruit always. You are rooted in overflow and grounded in greatness. Blessed permanently! You don't care about the year's drought, because He cares for you.

This is the reason why Jesus took over Jairus' case. That is why you don't hear Jairus saying anything, because the Lord took over everything. When the Lord takes over everything, you don't need to say anything. Just surrender to the Master.

Nothing is Impossible to Those who Believe

Jesus commanded that the girl should be given some meat to eat. What was previously impossible because of her condition was now totally healed, she needed to begin to live and to breathe and eat normally again. He did not call for her to be given milk such as would be given to a new born baby. No, Jesus called for meat to be provided. Meat is evidence of a maturity both in the physical realm and in spiritual symbolism. When God raises you up He is not raising you as a helpless infant. Your season of delay along the way has nurtured you and you are now a mature man or woman of God who has broken through into new levels of faith.

They Were Astonished

Even though Jesus had injected faith into Jairus for this resurrection miracle, still the Scriptures tell us that he and his wife were astonished. The story ended in astonishment in everyone who was there and all those who heard about it. Even until now we are all astonished and amazed at what Christ did to Jairus' daughter. Putting into consideration that she wasn't the first one to die in that village, but she was the first one to be resurrected from the dead.

It was heard for the first time that the daughter of Jairus was raised from the dead. It's my prayer that Christ may do something to you that will be the first to be recorded in your history records and in the records of those around you.

It was a great fight that Jairus' had to fight but it was worth it in the end. Don't give up this fight of faith. God wants do to some things in us but are we ready to take Him to our homes? Jesus will always surprise us with the extent of His goodness and kindness in our circumstances when we purpose to take Jesus home.

Jesus charged them not to tell anyone. It takes wisdom to know how and when to share what God has done in our lives and in the lives of those we love. We might feel like putting it all over Facebook or Twitter but sometimes we are to be like Mary, who treasured all things in her heart until their appointed time.

It's Possible for Your Story to Change

There are issues that have been going on in many families, that many people call family ties or family spirits or family beliefs. People in such families have totally come to believe in such theories and accepted them to be a part of their life.

Yet on the contrary when Jesus is invited to take over those families things completely change. So you don't have to make quick conclusions about your life and family before Jesus comes in. Allow Jesus to take over and let Him begin a new life for you.

Jairus is a very practical example to us. Do what he did and you will receive what he received.

There are so many things that Jesus can change in our lives if we can only allow Him. It's possible for your story to change no matter what it was before. Jesus is the only solution to every condition. Even to those life conditions that you have totally given up on. Don't bury it until Jesus first speaks to it.

Remember, every situation dead or alive hears when Jesus speaks. Jesus is the last Commander in Chief. Don't you ever make last decisions for yourself by yourself. Trust Jesus always, you will never be disappointed. Take Jesus in your family because He has the power and authority to change it all for you.

Ladies and gentlemen, our time of looking at and learning from the miracle of Jairus and the woman who bled is now drawing to a close. It is my prayer that this book has helped you to rise to a new level of faith for your own personal circumstances and that whatever you or a loved one may be facing and passing through that you can now see that Jesus is faithful in all and that He is going to help you to be a victor in your situation. You are going to live a better life because you are choosing to take your Jesus home.

Take Jesus Home

The name Jairus in Hebrew means "*Jehovah enlightens*". God opened up Jairus' heart and mind to receive a new level of resurrection faith. Make your mind up to take Jesus home just as Jairus did, and let him be your example. Put aside all your pride and humbly ask Jesus to come and help you. Just focus on Jesus and on His word of faith for your situation not on any other messages that may come to distract, delay or diminish your faith.

Don't allow messengers of negativity to derail you on your destiny path with Christ. Remember that in delay Jesus is preparing you for a greater blessing and He is saving the best for last. Don't be upset when another person receives their miracle before you receive yours. It is coming in Jesus' name and your waiting period is creating a greater platform for a bigger miracle in your life.

If Jesus blesses another person along the way, then He is helping you towards a greater anointing and blessing in your dilemma. Don't be jealous of their miracle, Rejoice in what Jesus is doing on the way for them. Delay is not a denial of the will of God in your life. Trust Jesus for His perfect timing and plans for your circumstances and BELIEVE ONLY IN HIM.

Let it be heard for the first time in your house that new things are emerging. The testimony of Christ's presence in your house cannot be resisted. It sounds beyond your borders; it's too much louder than the sound of your voice that it shouts by itself. That's why Jesus told them not to tell anyone about it – meaning it could talk for itself.

He will answer your prayers and raise you up higher than you can dare to dream.

God bless you today and always.

Apostle Stephen Kato,
New Destiny Ministries

ABOUT THE AUTHOR

"TWIN MINISTRY – NEW DESTINY MINISTRIES"

[18] Remember ye not the former things, neither consider the things of old.
[19] Behold, I will do a new thing; now it shall spring forth; shall ye not know it? I will even make a way in the wilderness, and rivers in the desert.
Isaiah 43

IDENTIFYING GOD'S PEOPLE TO THE NEW DESTINY THAT GOD HAS FOR THEM

Stephen Kato (top right), along with his twin brother **Godfrey Waswa** (top left) are the Co-Founders and International Directors of "***Twin Ministry – New Destiny Ministries***" based in Kampala, Uganda, East Africa. *New Destiny Ministries* is a multi-cultural, multi-racial, Holy Spirit filled, Word-based cutting edge Kingdom apostolic ministry. It has global influence and has made a powerful impact through an extensive relational network in many nations including Australia, Uganda, Tanzania, Kenya, Rwanda, Ghana, Hong Kong, Nepal, Nigeria, Malawi, DRC, Lesotho, South Africa, Zimbabwe, Zambia; London, Birmingham, Scotland, Northern Ireland, North Wales (UK); Sweden, Canada and numerous states throughout the USA including California, Florida, Hawaii, Los Angeles, New York, Maryland, Massachusetts, Missouri, Ohio, Pennsylvania, Virginia and Washington. They pastor a church called New Destiny Christian Centre in Kamuli, Uganda. Additionally, they have another church in Los Angeles, California.

The twins were radically saved in 1985 and since that time have been used by God in spreading the Gospel message of hope and restoration to the weary, to sinners, to saints and to servants of God alike. *New Destiny Ministries* regularly conduct revival and restoration meetings, leadership gatherings, seminars and crusades with which they spread the Gospel of Jesus Christ and the message that God has put upon their hearts. They work with many different churches, organizations, ministries and business people to contribute to the development of God's people and are committed to improving living conditions of humanity, to discipling God's people and to building His church. The ministry has a church plant in Kamuli, with exciting plans for a brand new mega-church plant in Kampala in the near future.

New Destiny Ministries have an extensive global radio and developing TV ministries. ***"Man of Destiny,"*** A best-selling book authored by *Stephen Kato*, is now available on-line and in paperback versions via Amazon and direct from the ministry. ***"Take Jesus Home***", Kato's second book is now also available on the global market. Both *Apostle Kato* and Apostle *Waswa* are sought after international teachers and preachers of the Word of God. They are men of integrity and humility whose apostolic ministries have been marked with signs and wonders following to the glory of God. *Kato* operates in a powerful breakthrough anointing especially in the area of faith miracles and finances. *Waswa* operates in a powerful breakthrough anointing in the area of teaching on God's government.

katotwin.sk@gmail.com
twinministry.weebly.com
New Destiny Ministries
P.O. Box 27576, Kampala, Uganda, East Africa
Stephen Kato: +256 788 176867; +254 728 468681
Godfrey Waswa: +1 (323) 736 7038 (USA) WhatsApp

OTHER BOOKS BY THE AUTHOR

"Man of Destiny" is a remarkable expose of God's heart for every believer. Kato skillfully opens the much-loved story of the Good Samaritan in a way never before seen to reveal God's power to restore and fulfil destiny in the lives of His own. If you have unanswered questions in your life you need look no further – the answer is in the narrative of Man of Destiny.

9 798638 419417